# DESERTS

Leon Gray

New York

Published in 2011 by The Rosen Publishing Group Inc.
29 East 21st Street, New York, NY 10010

Copyright © 2011 Wayland/
The Rosen Publishing Group, Inc.

First Edition

Editorial Director: Rasha Elsaeed
Editor: Katie Powell
Designer: Tim Mayer, Mayer Media
Illustrator: Peter Bull Art Studio
Consultant: Meg Gillett

Library of Congress Cataloging-in-Publication Data

Gray, Leon, 1974-
Deserts / by Leon Gray. -- 1st ed.
    p. cm. -- (Geography wise)
Includes index.
ISBN 978-1-4488-3280-4 (library binding)
1. Deserts--Juvenile literature. 2. Desert ecology--Juvenile literature.
3. Desert animals--Juvenile literature. 4. Desert plants--Juvenile literature. I. Title.
GB612.G735 2011
551.41'5--dc22
                        2010023797

Photographs:
Title page © Istock, imprint and contents page background © Shutterstock, p. 4(t&b) © Istock,
p. 5 © Wayland, p. 6 © Juan Carlos Munoz/naturepl.com p. 7(t) © Wayland, p. 7(b) © Istock,
p. 8 © Istock, p. 9 (t) © L.Clarke/CORBIS, p. 9(c&b) © Shutterstock, p. 10 © Getty Images, p. 11
and cover © Kazuyoshi Nomachi/Corbis, p. 12/13 © Bob Krist/CORBIS, p. 13(t) © Fred Olivier/
naturepl.com, p. 14 © John Noble/CORBIS, p. 15(l) © Istock, p. 15 © NASA/Corbis, p. 16 ©
Istock, p. 17 © Istock, p. 18(t&b) © Istock, p. 19(t&b) © Shutterstock, p. 20© Istock, p. 21 ©
Shutterstock, p. 22 © Istock, p. 23(t) © Istock, p. 23(b) © George Steinmetz/Corbis, p. 24 ©
Istock, p. 25 © Peter Turnley/CORBIS, p. 26 © NASA/Science Photo Library, p. 27 © Science
Source/Science Photo Library, p. 28 (t) © Istock, p. 28 (b) © Shutterstock, p. 29 (tr) © Istock,
p. 29 (tl, cr, cl& bl) © Shutterstock.

Manufactured in China
CPSIA Compliance Information: Batch #WAW1102PK: For Further Information
contact Rosen Publishing, New York, New York at 1-800-237-9932

# Contents

# What Are Deserts?

A desert is any place that gets less than 10 inches (25 centimeters) of **precipitation** in an average year. Deserts cover around 25 percent of the Earth's land surface area. They include very hot places, such as the Sahara in Africa, and very cold places, such as Antarctica and Greenland, which are "dry" because the precipitation falls as snow and never melts.

Deserts may seem barren but some animals and plants have learned to cope with the harsh conditions and lack of water. People also live in the desert. The Bedouin and Tuareg lead traditional, **nomadic** lives, and other people live in big cities that have been built in the middle of deserts, such as Cairo in Egypt. Deserts also hold rich natural resources, which are very useful to people.

*The Sahara is a huge, sandy desert that stretches across most of North Africa.*

*The Sonoran Desert is a rocky desert that straddles the border between Mexico and the United States.*

4

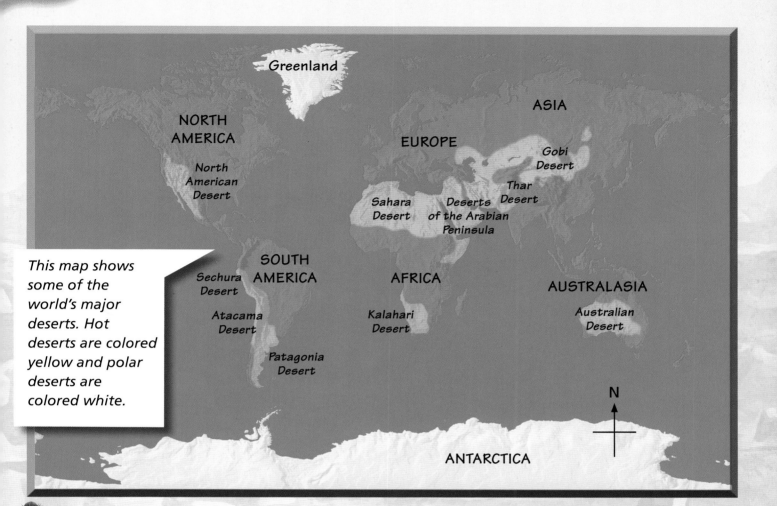

This map shows some of the world's major deserts. Hot deserts are colored yellow and polar deserts are colored white.

# THE WORLD'S BIGGEST DESERTS

| Desert | Continent | Area (sq. miles) | Area (sq. km) |
| --- | --- | --- | --- |
| Antarctica | Antarctica | 5,500,000 | 14,200,000 |
| Sahara | Africa | 3,320,000 | 8,600,000 |
| Arabian | Asia | 900,000 | 2,330,000 |
| Greenland | Europe | 677,676 | 1,755,637 |
| Gobi | Asia | 500,000 | 1,300,000 |
| Kalahari | Africa | 360,000 | 930,000 |
| Patagonian | South America | 260,000 | 673,000 |
| Rub' al-Khali | Asia | 250,000 | 650,000 |
| Great Victoria | Australia | 250,000 | 647,000 |
| Great Basin | North America | 190,000 | 492,000 |
| Chihuahuan | North America | 175,000 | 450,000 |

*Source: http://www.britannica.com*

# How Do Deserts Form?

There are a lot of deserts just north and south of the **equator**. This is because the Sun shines very strongly at the equator. Its heat warms the air, which rises and then cools. When this happens, any water vapor in the cool air turns into liquid water and falls as rain. The cool, dry air then spreads north and south to the **tropics** and slowly sinks. Since there is no water in the air, these places are very dry.

Many deserts form in the middle of large areas of land, far from seas and oceans. So any rain falls from the clouds long before it reaches the middle of the land. Other deserts form in the shelter of mountains. When damp air meets a mountain, it rises. Clouds form because damp air cools as it rises. The water then falls as precipitation.

Some deserts form in the **rain shadow** of a mountain. Look at the diagram on the next page to see why this happens.

Rain falls on slopes facing
wet ocean winds

Desert

Where moist winds blow toward a mountain,
most rain falls on the nearest slope. The far side,
called the **rain shadow**, gets very little rain.

By the time the air reaches the peak, all the moisture
in it has already fallen. So the air on the far side of the
mountain is dry and deserts are more likely to form there.

Occasionally deserts are found on the coast, next to
the sea. This happens because **ocean currents** bring
very cold water close to the shore, cooling the air
above it. Cold air cannot carry much water, so any
winds that blow inland off the sea are very dry.

The Namib Desert
stretches along the
Atlantic coast of
Namibia in Africa.

# Rocky Deserts

Most deserts are rocky places covered with boulders and loose stones. Rocky deserts form when the topsoil dries out. The wind then blows the soil away to expose the **bedrock** below.

The wind is an important force in the desert. As the wind blows away the soil, it creates a lot of dust. The wind picks up particles of dust and cuts patterns and ridges in boulders and other rocks. This process is called **erosion**.

## UNBELIEVABLE!

Chemicals in some desert rocks react with the dry air to form a light brown to black coating called "desert varnish."

*These cliffs have formed as layers of sand are buried and pressed down to form sandstone rock. The desert winds erode the sandstone into amazing rock formations.*

Many of the typical features of rocky deserts are the result of wind erosion.

• A **mesa** is a large plateau of rock with a flat top, like Ayers Rock in Australia. The wind does not erode the top layer of harder rock, which protects softer rocks below from erosion.

• A **rock pedestal** is a mushroom-shaped rock. These rocks gradually develop because more dust blows near the surface of the ground. So the rock wears away more quickly near the ground, creating an unusual, mushroom-shaped rock.

• A **yardang** is a long ridge of bare rock created when much softer rocks on either side of it are removed by wind erosion.

# Sandy Deserts

Sandy deserts form when the wind erodes soft rock at Earth's surface. This rock crumbles into tiny particles of sand, which blows over the land.

Sand covers about 25 percent of all the deserts in the world. Sand **dunes** cover these desert lands, forming "sand seas" or **ergs**. The dunes form because the wind blows the sand into different shapes. Barchan dunes are crescent shaped.

Dome dunes are circular heaps of sand, and linear, seif dunes are long, narrow ridges of sand.

Sand dunes slowly move over the land in a similar way to waves moving across the sea. The wind blows sand up the slope of the dune. The sand then collects on the other side. Most sand dunes move around 65 to 100 feet (20 to 30 meters) in one year.

## R. A. BAGNOLD

The first person to study sand dunes was the British army officer Ralph Bagnold (1896–1990). He went out into the Sahara to study its dunes and wrote a book about them. Space scientists used his book to study sand dunes on Mars.

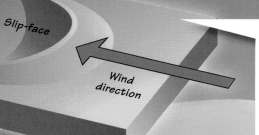

Barchan dunes form when the wind blows mainly from one direction. The dune moves as wind transports sand up the dune's steep slope until it reaches the top. The sand is then deposited along the slip-face of the dune. Over time, this moves the whole dune forward in the direction the wind blows.

The wind blows the sands of the Sahara into giant dunes, which tower over the nomads who live there.

# Ice Deserts

The term *desert* includes Antarctica and areas around the North Pole—in Greenland and northern parts of North America and Asia.

These "ice deserts" are so bitterly cold that all the water is frozen. Although snow is usually the only form of precipitation, it can sometimes rain during the very short summer season.

## UNBELIEVABLE!

Many sources will tell you that the Sahara is the world's biggest desert. They do not include Antarctica as a true desert. But Antarctica covers 5.5 million square miles (14.2 million sq. km) of land—nearly twice the size of the Sahara.

*The ice desert of Antarctica is the coldest, driest, and windiest place on the planet.*

Although the temperature of ice deserts is very different to that of hot, dry deserts, the landscapes are very similar. Both are barren places and few animals and plants can survive there. Most of the water is permanently frozen, so there is very little to drink.

Sometimes, ice deserts are found at high altitude in mountain regions. The air here is usually dry because any water in it has already fallen as rain or snow lower down the slopes. All the water there occurs as ice and snow because of the freezing temperatures at high altitude.

*Male emperor penguins huddle together while they keep their eggs warm during the bitter Antarctic winter.*

# Weather in Deserts

Weather varies from desert to desert. The temperature can range from very hot to very cold. Hot deserts often become cold at night. During the day, the strong sunlight heats up the bare rock and sand very quickly. However, without clouds to trap the daytime heat, the rock and sand cool very quickly at night.

The lack of water and these extremes of temperature mean that most trees and plants cannot grow in deserts. Without plant cover to slow the wind, deserts tend to be windy places. In sandy deserts, strong winds can whip up **sandstorms**. In ice deserts, they can cause blizzards.

*A fierce blizzard blows around a tent at a camp on Butson Point, a northeast glacier in Antarctica.*

Sometimes desert winds spin around in a tight circle, whipping up particles of sand and dust like a mini-tornado. The rapidly rotating column of air is called a **dust devil** (left).

Some deserts have seasons. The Gobi Desert and Patagonia Desert are hot in the summer, but freezing cold in the winter. Other deserts have a long dry season and a short rainy season. When it does rain in a desert, a lot of water falls in a very short period of time. This often causes **flash floods** because the ground surface has become so hard during months of continuous hot, dry weather, that it cannot soak up the huge amount of water that falls so quickly.

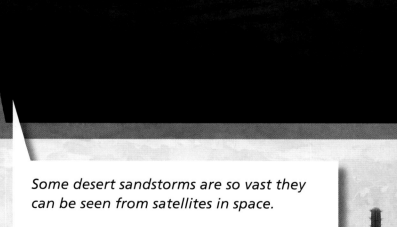

*Some desert sandstorms are so vast they can be seen from satellites in space.*

15

# Where Is the Water?

Although all deserts are dry, there is usually some water there. Water is everywhere in ice deserts, but it is frozen as ice and snow. In hot deserts, most of the water is in rocks deep under the ground. Sometimes this water bubbles up to the surface as an **oasis**.

*An oasis is a vital source of water for all the animals, plants, and people that live in the desert.*

*Rocks line the banks of a dried-up riverbed, or wadi. The wadi fills with water only during times of heavy rainfall.*

Some deserts get water during a rainy season or when sudden storms occur. Sometimes rivers can form after heavy rainfall but then disappear just as quickly. Their water flows in channels called **wadis**, which are completely dry for the rest of the year.

In coastal deserts, dew is a vital source of water. At night, hot air from the desert rises. This pulls in air from the sea, bringing with it much needed water in the form of water vapor. Desert plants collect this water in the air as dew.

# UNBELIEVABLE!

Sometimes people think they can see water in the desert, but really, it is light playing a trick on them. In the desert, hot air can bend light from the blue sky so it looks like water on the ground. This is called a **mirage**.

# Desert Wildlife

Life on Earth cannot exist without water. The animals and plants that live in deserts have ways to cope with the lack of water and the hot and cold temperatures. This is called **adaptation**.

Since there is little soil in the desert, any rain that falls soaks quickly into the ground. Many desert plants have long, branching roots that "tap" into underground water. They are called "taproots."

Other plants sprout from seed, grow, and flower very quickly during the short rainy season. Most plants lose water through their leaves, so desert plants have small leaves, like the spines of cacti, or no leaves at all.

*This web-footed gecko in the Namib Desert keeps its feet cool by running very quickly across the sand.*

*Plants called cacti grow in the deserts of North America. They store water in huge stems, which can swell up to hold more water.*

*The enormous ears of the fennec fox help this desert predator to keep cool. Its thick fur keeps the fox warm during the cold nights.*

Most desert animals sleep to avoid the heat during the day. Animals that are active at night are called nocturnal animals. They include small mammals such as gerbils and jerboas, as well as predators such as the fennec fox. Some animals never drink water—they get all they need from their food. Others drink the dew that collects on desert plants.

# UNBELIEVABLE!

Camels can survive for up to seven days without water and several months without food in the hot desert. They do this by burning the fat stored in their humps to get the energy they need, and they take in moisture from the food they've eaten. When they do reach a source of water, a single camel can drink more than 44 gallons (200 liters) of water at one time!

# Living in the Desert

People have been living in deserts for thousands of years. Some are nomads; this means they wander across the desert, herding animals such as camels and goats for food and liquids. The Bedouin of the Arabian Desert are nomads. Traditionally, they live in tents made from camel skins. These tents stay cool during the day and keep in the warmth at night. The Bedouin also cover up from the hot Sun by wearing lots of clothes.

*The Bedouin have lived traditional nomadic lives in the Arabian Desert for thousands of years. Recently, with the discovery of oil, some have chosen to settle into a more Western way of life.*

*The world's biggest desert city is Cairo in Egypt. It is home to more than 10 million people.*

Some desert people, such as those in the Kalahari of Southern Africa, lead hunter-gatherer lifestyles. They hunt desert mammals and collect food such as fruits and eggs. Others choose to settle in one place. Nomads, such as the Bedouin, set up temporary villages near an oasis, moving on after a few months. Others make more permanent homes, building houses from mud and stone.

Some deserts are now home to modern cities. Examples include Las Vegas in Nevada and Riyadh in Saudi Arabia. Dams and pipelines have to be built to supply enough water for everyone. This is expensive, so desert cities are usually only found in rich countries.

# Using Deserts

Deserts often have valuable natural resources underground. **Crude oil** is one of the most important of these. Oil is buried deep under the ground in the Arabian Desert. Crude oil is **refined** to provide fuel for airplanes, cars, and for power stations, which generate electricity.

Important rocks and minerals are also found in many deserts. Sandstone and granite are important building materials. Sand is used to make concrete and glass, and precious metals and gems, such as diamonds, occur underground in some deserts.

*Deserts may seem like barren places, but some hide a valuable resource—crude oil. This oil refinery in the Arabian Desert processes crude oil into fuel.*

Many people go to deserts to see beautiful landscapes—such as the Grand Canyon in Arizona. Other people enjoy sightseeing at monuments such as the pyramids in Egypt. People may visit deserts to try new sports, such as sand surfing and dune rallying.

*The ancient pyramids make Cairo in Egypt and its surrounding desert one of the top **tourist** destinations in the world.*

# DESERT ENERGY

Deserts are ideal places to build **solar power plants** and wind farms. Solar power plants collect energy from the bright desert sunlight. **Wind farms** generate energy from the strong desert winds.

***Irrigation** systems feed water through pipes and drip lines so people can grow alfalfa crops in Saudi Arabia.*

# Dangerous Deserts

Deserts can be dangerous places for people. In ice deserts, **frostbite** is a common danger when parts of the body, such as the fingers, freeze. People need to wear the right clothes to trap heat and insulate the body.

In hot deserts, people can suffer from **heat stroke**. This is when your body temperature rises too quickly and you cannot sweat and cool down. At night, it can be so cold that **hypothermia** is a threat. This is when your body temperature falls below 95°F (35°C). Since there is very little water in the hot desert, **dehydration** is another danger. This is when your body does not get enough water.

*People who live in or near deserts sometimes struggle to get enough water to drink. **Droughts** also cause food shortages because there is not enough water to grow crops.*

# RACE AGAINST TIME

In 1910, Captain Robert Scott (1868–1912) led a team of British explorers in a race to the South Pole. Scott and his team arrived at the South Pole in January 1912. His rival, Roald Amundsen (1872–1928) from Norway, had already gotten there. Scott and his colleagues died on their way back across Antarctica.

People who live in deserts with wet seasons rely on the water to survive. A drought can occur if the rain does not arrive. People may then not have enough water to drink. They may also go hungry because there is no water to grow crops for food.

Desert weather can also be dangerous. Desert winds can create swirling sandstorms, which make it difficult to see. People may die if they get lost in a sandstorm.

*This sandstorm in Jordan is making it hard for these men to see where they are walking. They have covered their faces to protect their skin from the flying sand.*

# Deserts: Good or Bad?

Satellite images have shown that many deserts are spreading. This process is called **desertification**. The wind plays a big role in the spread of deserts, but people's activities are also to blame.

Some farmers who live on the edges of deserts are letting their livestock overgraze the land. Plant roots hold the soil together and keep in water. When plants are eaten away by animals grazing, the soil breaks apart and deserts start to spread. This means there is less land to grow crops and keep livestock.

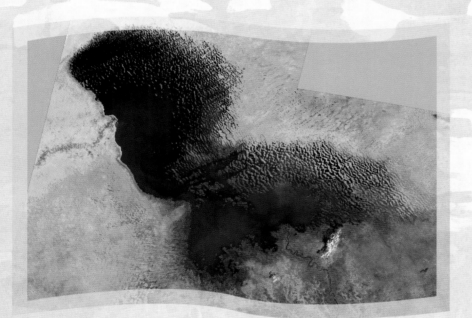

*In under 40 years, Lake Chad in the Sahel region south of the Sahara has shrunk to less than 5 percent of its original size. The satellite image top left shows Lake Chad as it was in 1973. The satellite image below shows Lake Chad in 2007.*

Many people think we should be protecting deserts rather than worrying about desertification. They think that mining, farming, tourism, and other activities are damaging deserts and desert wildlife.

There are some countries with deserts that have laws to protect desert animals and plants. They also have laws to stop people from using too much water.

*Scientists study the climate in deserts to learn more about desertification and to help predict natural disasters, such as droughts and sandstorms.*

# UNBELIEVABLE!

The Romans were once able to grow fruits and vines across much of North Africa, now covered by the Sahara Desert.

# Exploring a Desert!

## Desert Features

The wind is an important force in the desert. It shapes many of a desert's typical features. Look at the two pictures on this page and see if you can find out how and why they have formed in the desert. You'll need to find out about the particular desert that the feature is found in, such as the weather conditions and the desert's surrounding area.

Rock pedestals form in rocky deserts such as the Mojave Desert, in California. How does the wind help to form these desert features?

Seif dunes are long, narrow ridges of sand found in sandy deserts such as the Sahara. How do these desert features form? How do other types of sand dunes form?

## Desert Adaptations

Take a look at the pictures of different animals and plants on this page. They are all adapted to life in the desert. Use the Internet to help you find the answers to the questions below.

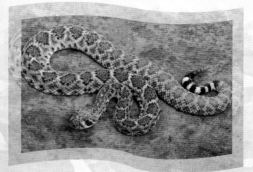

• The western diamondback rattlesnake lives in which of the world's deserts? Why do you think this predator hunts at night?

• The saguaro cactus plant is found in which deserts around the world? How is it adapted to life in the desert?

• *Welwitschia mirabilis* is a plant that grows in the Namib Desert of southern Africa. How can it survive in the heat of the desert?

• How does the namib desert beetle get the water it needs to survive in the desert?

• How does the golden cartwheeling spider protect itself when it feels threatened?

## Living in the Desert

People live in deserts, too. Use the Internet to find out more about the Tuareg people of North Africa. Imagine you are living with a Tuareg family. Write a story or keep a journal to document your own experience.

Discover more about oil exploration in Arabian deserts. In which deserts has oil been found? How is the oil extracted? You could write a newspaper article explaining the positives and negatives of oil exploration in a desert.

# Cross-Curricular Links

Use this topic web to investigate deserts in other parts of your curriculum.

**English & IT**
Use the Internet or books at your local library to find out about the Tuareg people of the Sahara. Write a story or poem to show how they cope with life in such a harsh environment.

**Citizenship**
Write a speech urging people to protect the world's deserts. What reasons would you give?

**Art**
Draw pictures of animals in the style of the Aborigines from the central desert (outback) of Australia.

# DESERTS

**Math**
Use an atlas or the Internet to calculate the distance between your school and the Sahara.

**History**
Use the Internet or books at your local library to investigate Captain Robert Scott's expedition to the South Pole. Write a diary in the words of Captain Scott to explain how he was feeling in the last few days of the ill-fated journey.

**Science**
Explore the feeding relationships between the different plants and animals that live in the desert. Draw a food web to show how they are related.

# Glossary

**Adaptation** A gradual process that occurs as a living being becomes better suited to its habitat.

**Bedrock** Solid rock that lies beneath Earth's surface.

**Crude oil** The raw material from which gasoline, kerosene, and other fuels are made.

**Dehydration** When the body does not get enough water.

**Desertification** When human activities and natural conditions, such as the wind, turn the land into a desert.

**Drought** When little or no rain falls.

**Dune** A mound of sand formed by the wind.

**Dust devil** A small, swirling mass of sand and air, like a mini-tornado.

**Equator** An imaginary line around Earth's surface, lying midway between the North and South Poles.

**Erg** A large, flat area of desert covered by windswept sand.

**Erosion** The wearing away of Earth's surface by water or the wind.

**Flash flood** A flood that rises quickly and without warning.

**Frostbite** When parts of the body, especially the fingers, face, and feet freeze when exposed to extreme cold.

**Heat stroke** When the core body temperature rises above 104°F (40°C) and the main organs start to shut down.

**Hypothermia** When the core body temperature drops below 95°F (35°C), causing serious health problems.

**Irrigation** To supply water through channels.

**Mesa** A large plateau of rock with a flat top.

**Mirage** An optical illusion where hot desert air bends light from the blue sky so it looks like water on the ground.

**Nomad** A person who has no permanent home and moves around according to the seasons.

**Oasis** A fertile area of desert land where water bubbles to the surface.

**Ocean current** The flow of water in an ocean.

**Precipitation** Water that falls as rain, hail, sleet, or snow.

**Rain shadow** An area that is dry because a mountain shields it from moist winds.

**Refine** To remove unwanted parts of crude oil to make fuel.

**Rock pedestal** A mushroom-shaped rock formed by wind erosion.

**Sandstorm** A strong desert wind that carries sand across the desert.

**Solar power plant** A power plant that generates electricity from the Sun's heat.

**Tourism** To travel for recreation or leisure.

**Tropics** Hot, humid regions near the equator.

**Wadi** A dried-up river channel that carries water during the rainy season.

**Wind farm** A power plant that generates electricity using wind turbines.

# Index

# Further Information

## Books

**Deserts and Polar Regions Around the World**
by Jen Green
(PowerKids Press, 2009)

**The World's Most Amazing Deserts**
by Anna Claybourne
(Heinemann-Raintree, 2009)

**Who Lives Here?: Desert Animals**
by Deborah Hodge
(Kids Can Press, 2008)

## Web Sites

Due to the changing nature of Internet links, PowerKids Press has developed an online list of Web sites related to the subject of this book. This site is updated regularly. Please use this link to access this list:
http://www.powerkidslinks.com/geo/deserts